THE BEAUTY ALCHEMIST

Valerie Cody

THE BEAUTY ALCHEMIST

DEDICATION

I dedicate this book to every person who believes in the power of self-transformation.

...to every person who seeks to understand the connection between mind, body, and soul.

...to every person who wishes to become the greatest version of themselves.

...to every person who has ever inspired me to be a more loving person.

...to every person who has ever inspired me to elevate my consciousness.

....to the people who have challenged my perspective and thus prompted my greatest awakenings.

...to the Source of all that is, was, and ever will be.

I dedicate this book to my eight-year-old self who wrote her first book in Mr. Olson's fourth grade class about Samoyed puppies.

TABLE OF CONTENTS

♦

INTRODUCTION

Dear One,

I wrote my first book when I was in fourth grade. Our assignment was to create a sequel to one of the books we had read as a class. Even though it has been many years since that assignment, I still remember what it was like to feel the words form at my fingertips and to create a new world through those words. This was when I knew someday I would be an author.

Here I am, decades later, bringing you my insight into what I have learned so far in my lifetime. In this book you will find offerings from my soul - ways to nourish your mind, body, and spirit. It is my sincere hope that these chapters unfold for you in a way that resonates deeply and leads to a more authentic and loving lifestyle.

Sometimes it takes years of resisting our heart's path just to realize all of the reasons we should follow it. During those years of resisting, we often find ourselves battling between our heart's calling and our worldly responsibilities. It becomes a constant stretching of our willpower to hold back from what we truly want, for what we 'think we should do.' But we all know, deep down, that the true heart's calling never fully goes away; in order to embrace this there must be healing.

As children, we believe in our dreams fully and we do not pollute them with doubt. But as we grow up those dreams become less bright, and they may even become a source of pain as we long after them.

Mostly, the resistance comes masked as self-doubt. We tell ourselves that we do not deserve what we truly want or we should wait…wait until our children are grown, until we find a life partner, until we lose weight, or until the tools we need arrive at our doorstep. Of course these are all illusions. All of our creative power lies in the present moment, not in the future.

This book is a testament to how someone (me) who resisted writing for decades through the lens of self-doubt, can implement the ideas discussed in these chapters and follow a dream.

In the past, I listened to my egoic mind and identified with the thoughts of self-loathing that circulated in my psyche. *For years.* As you may know from your own experience, that form of identification leaks into our daily lives in subtle ways. We end up self-sabotaging our efforts by choosing foods that do not offer health, partners that do not offer love, jobs that do not offer fulfillment, etc. **As a by-product of this, we do not offer our best foot forward into the world; we become a watered-down version of ourselves.**

This moment is different though. Right now you hold in your hands the treasure map that I followed, which lead me to the realization that I **can** follow my heart's desire. It is my hope that you will find at least one practice, perspective, recipe, or idea that can help you along your own path.

It is true that the world needs your embodied self, your true self, and your powerful self. It is true that the world needs your soul's offering.

-Valerie Cody

GOALS

"The greater danger for most of us lies not in setting our aim too high and falling short; but in setting our aim too low, and achieving our mark."— Michelangelo

Use this section to write down the dreams and goals you wish to achieve this year. Hold nothing back and write down the first thoughts that come to mind. All dreams are valid.

1.

2.

3.

4.

5.

6.

7.

8.

9.

10.

<u>GOALS</u>

"Pleasure in the job puts perfection in the work."
-Aristotle

11.

12.

13.

14.

15.

16.

17.

18.

19.

20.

21.

22.

THE BEGINNING IS THE MOST IMPORTANT
PART OF THE WORK.

-PLATO

Chapter One

WHAT IS ALCHEMY?

In the history of science, the term "alchemy" refers to both an early investigation of nature and an early form of spiritual discipline. This practice combined elements of chemistry, physics, medicine, astrology, mysticism, spirituality, and artistic expression. Philosophical systems and networks of educational facilities with the mission of studying alchemy span at least 2500 years and many continents. Geographically, alchemy was prevalent throughout Mesopotamia, Persia, India, China, Ancient Egypt, Classical Rome and Greece, and in Muslim civilization. More recently, Europeans of the 19th century practiced and upheld alchemical traditions.

In today's world, similar investigations of the natural world are deemed "scientific." Thus, certain aspects of alchemy can be viewed as the precursor to modern science. As the centuries have passed, the perception of alchemists has become one of pseudo-science.

Indeed, some practitioners of alchemy were dishonest with their attempts of turning lead into gold and concocting magic potions and miraculous remedies. As with any profession, there are certain individuals who do not truly represent the proper manifestation of the profession - and alchemists of olde were no different.

However, these types of practitioners made up the minority and most alchemists were well-meaning and distinguished scientists like Robert Boyle and Isaac Newton. These early thinkers explored the natural world via experimentation, traditional processes, and the scientific method as they uncovered the mysteries of physicality.

For the most part, the conquest of literally turning base metals such as lead, into the most valuable substance - gold - was a legitimate profession and veritable mission. While this may be the original definition and goal of this term, in this book we are going to apply the virtues of alchemy in a metaphorical, philosophical, and spiritual way.

For example, we will allow the concept of "lead into gold" to be the foundation for the spiritual practice of refinement that turns our darkest and least desirable thoughts, words, and actions (lead) into love (gold).

We will also work in the kitchen, using simple and everyday ingredients (lead) to create delicious and nutritious fare (gold). Furthermore, I will provide 'alchemical' recipes for beauty treatments using natural ingredients from the Earth such as clay (lead) and turn them into the lavish royal beauty treatments of ancient times (gold).

◆

EAT YOUR BEST
FEEL YOUR BEST
LOOK YOUR BEST

Chapter Two

THE HUMAN BODY: MASTER ALCHEMIST

Powerful allegorical references can be found in the study of alchemy. In the previous chapter, we discussed how the tangible aspects of the alchemical process work to transform base metals into gold. Here is how the human body works as a master alchemist to keep us living our best lives:

<u>Digestion:</u> When we eat food, it is transformed into metabolic energy for our bodies. We even measure the amount of energy found in foods by using the word 'calorie.' The body is acting as an alchemist in this context without our conscious knowing or effort. Through the process of digestion, the food we ingest

is being chemically transformed into the very life-force that keeps us alive, full of energy, and functioning properly.

In order to be the healthiest and most vibrant version of ourselves, proper digestion is key. We can look to Ayurvedic knowledge as we work to be more conscious of the inner-workings of our bodies. We can look at the definitions used to describe the quality of digestion in the body. These terms also spread far beyond the simple way I am describing them here, but in any case we can certainly see the correlation and point of bringing these into the conversation.

Agni: is a Sanskrit word meaning fire, and connotes the Vedic fire god of Hinduism. This term is also used to describe the digestive fire within the body. In the world of Ayurvedic Medicine, healthy Agni is the key to optimal health. It digests our food, processes our emotions, and oversees intelligence throughout the body. Agni is one of the most critical factors in determining overall health.

Ama: is the antithesis of Agni. It is toxic, slow moving sludge that can accumulate within the tissues and digestive tract of an unhealthy body. This substance is a form of un-metabolized waste that cannot be used by the body. The word itself means **"uncooked, immature, undigested"** and this substance is a result of impaired Agni or digestive fire. In this way, impaired Agni and accumulated Ama enter into a self-perpetuating cycle that when left unchecked can be the root of many ailments.

The normal process of consuming food looks like this:

<u>Step 1:</u> All the food we eat is fully digested.

<u>Step 2:</u> Much of the food we eat is absorbed into the body as nutrients and the rest exits the body as waste products.

However, this may not always be the case due to stress, disease in the body, improper food combining, not eating seasonally, or consuming toxic and unhealthy food. <u>Ama</u> is formed in the body when a portion of the food-matter can be classified as neither nutrients nor waste products. Over time, this in-between substance builds up in the tissues of the body and impairs the body's ability to perform optimally.

Characteristics of Agni:

- ◆Sharp
- ◆Light
- ◆Dry
- ◆Subtle
- ◆Clear
- ◆Hot

Characteristics of Ama:

- ◆Dull
- ◆Heavy
- ◆Oily
- ◆Viscous
- ◆Wet
- ◆Stagnant
- ◆Cold

This material does, indeed, accumulate in the digestive system due to poorly digested food, but it will spread deeper into the bodily tissues when not balanced with proper Agni. Too much Ama will disrupt the bio-availability of the nutrients we are consuming and lead to malnourished cells. When Ama spreads deeper into the cell membranes, coating them, it inhibits cellular communication and weakens immune response.

In order to recognize how and when we need to use our inner-alchemy to bring fire into our bodies, we need to be able to recognize when the Agni-Ama balance has been disrupted.

Physical and Mental Symptoms of Excess Ama:

• Feeling energetically "heavy"

• Slow and stagnant digestion

• Sinus congestion

• Stagnation in career, life-goals, or ambition

• Sexual dysfunction or low sex drive

• Poor appetite

• Tastebuds seem muted or food tastes abnormal

• Lack of mental clarity

• Thick white coating on the tongue

• Dullness in the eyes

• Feeling weak

• Acne

• Low self-esteem

• Depression, anxiety, or fear of the unknown

• Brain fog

• Weight gain

If you feel that you have accumulated excess Ama in your body, it will be necessary to make changes in your lifestyle in order to achieve optimal health. A personalized consultation with an Ayurvedic practitioner should be a part of your healing journey.

♦

Foods and Lifestyle Habits That Increase Ama:

♦ Cheese

♦ Meat

♦ Expired food

♦ Reheated food (leftovers)

♦ Nightshade vegetables (tomatoes, potatoes, peppers)

♦ Fried foods

♦ Going to bed late

♦ Waking up late

♦ Eating large portions of food after sunset

♦ Eating while emotionally distressed

♦ Irregular eating habits

♦ Eating passed the feeling of comfortable satiety

♦ A generally sedentary lifestyle

♦ Cold and wet climates

<u>Foods and Lifestyle Habits That Increase Agni:</u>

♦ Grapefruit

♦ Nuts and seeds (<u>must</u> be sprouted)

♦ Ginger

♦ Garlic

♦ Sweating through physical exercise

♦ Using an infrared sauna

♦ Waking at sunrise

♦ Breathing deeply

♦ Properly combining food during meals

♦ Eating when the sun is high in the sky

♦ Practicing yoga

♦ Dry-brushing

♦ Rebounding

♦ Warm and dry climates

TENDING TO YOUR INNER BEAUTY WILL
REFLECT IN YOUR OUTER BEAUTY.

Chapter Three

SPIRITUAL ALCHEMY

A legitimate science until the 1800's, alchemy was practiced by some of the most notable figures in scientific history such as Isaac Newton, Roger Bacon, Nicholas Flamel, and Saint Thomas Aquinas. These men were mysterious, otherworldly, and often times eccentric. Alchemists were hired by nobles to work day and night in search of a way to turn common metals in gold, and some are rumored to have succeeded. But these scientific wizards were also in search of something else: a substance that would make a person healthy, wealthy and wise to an extreme degree. This substance is known as The Philosopher's Stone.

From a bird's eye view, one could see how these two goals are actually quite related. In both scenarios the alchemist takes something common and transforms it into something extraordinary.

In scenario one, the alchemist transforms a common metal into the most valuable substance of the ages. In scenario two, the alchemist creates an elixir that will transform a common person into someone of constant health (never aging), unimaginable riches (unlimited power and resources), and God-like intelligence (the ability to wield this power). Thus, making this person unquestionable and all-powerful.

While these aspirations may be interesting and worthwhile to some, the spiritual aspirant finds the real gem within the process of spiritual alchemy. In **spiritual alchemy,** we can see yet another parallel: Turn all negative experiences, emotions and actions into the one universal power and truth: *Love*.

This is our mission here on Earth.

Spiritual alchemy is a system of processes that lead the seeker to release old paradigms and move forward to a radical new perspective. The spiritual-seeker becomes the alchemist when he or she realizes that the power to transform oneself lies within, because the power of God lives within us all. The transformative process of alchemizing our negative thoughts, experiences, and emotions into gold (love) comes from a determination to advance spiritually on our own unique paths.

This is the seven step process of spiritual alchemy:

1. Calcination: Alchemists like Newton began the process of scientific alchemy by heating and decomposing raw matter. Spiritually, this first step represents the defragmenting of our self-doubt and self-sabotaging habits. We start to lift the veil of pride and arrogance, discovering what is really driving these behaviors and patterns.

2. Dissolution: The second step begins once we have broken down the characteristics of our personality that may have been blocking us from spiritual maturity. Dissolution represents an awareness of self that has been freed from false pride and ego. This process allows us to see the greater picture and view our positive and negative qualities objectively. Here is where we start to take ownership of our faults, negative mindset, and less than favorable actions. All of the trauma we have been avoiding, pain that has been stuffed down for years, and unsavory memories will bubble up to the surface. We will consciously have to face these challenges and in doing so, we gain awareness of how our actions may be affecting the world around us and other people. It should be noted that this step might happen spontaneously or accidentally through serious illness or other life changing experiences.

3. Separation: If you have any prior experience with spiritual work, this step is closely related to 'Shadow Work.' The third step is where we sort through our thoughts and emotions. We become truly aware of our authentic feelings

for others and ourselves. We face our inner anger, sadness, and frustration - we face off with our shadow self. In this work, we do not have the luxury of dealing with these things the way we may have been before (working too hard, eating too much, spending too much money, abusing drugs, sex or alcohol). No, this time we must unwind the habits and allow them to literally come out of the shadows and into the light. Doing this will isolate particular elements of our personality that need to be honestly assessed and viewed objectively.

4. Conjunction: The first three steps have been about purification. In the fourth step of spiritual alchemy, we are simmering everything that is left; here is when we work to accept our true and authentic selves. Conjunction is the process of allowing everything that bubbled up from our subconscious to be released into the light.

5. Fermentation: Fermentation marks the beginning of our rebirth. While we have been working through aspects of our old personalities during steps one through four, step five sees us beginning to experience moments of refinement. Two parts exist here: Putrefaction and Spiritization. We dissolved parts of our old selves that did not serve us and we experienced an inner death of our false self, this is *putrefaction*. Next, we released much of what has held us back in the past and the world can be seen in a new light, this is *spiritization*. Moments of deep inner peace and calmness will manifest here.

6. <u>Distillation:</u> Step six in spiritual alchemy is the integration of these spiritual realizations into our daily lives. The goal is to allow our new self to become permanent, and our new perspective to completely overshadow our old perspective. This is a deeper level of purification and we are truly becoming embodied into the the changes we have been making. Here is where we can zero in on the present moment, and become consciously aware of which 'self' we are letting drive. We die and are reborn in every conscious moment - going through steps 1-5 every moment until we have reached a state of purification that exists as 'enlightenment.' Literally, bringing our conscious awareness into the light.

7. <u>Coagulation:</u> Here we have arrived at the seventh and final step of spiritual alchemy. This is where we have liberated ourselves completely from attachment to the mind, and have become totally embodied into our soul. The moment the soul becomes one with the Source of all consciousness, it becomes totally self-aware. Duality does not exist and the manifested world is not separate from the mind; rather it is a reflection of it.

◆

A PHYSICAL TRANSFORMATION CAN ONLY COME AFTER A SPIRITUAL TRANSFORMATION.

Chapter Four

YOUR HIGHER SELF

When we came into this world, we separated from Source Energy in order to experience life as a human, balance karma, and grow spiritually. While we are ever-connected to Source (and never fully separated) a larger part of us still exists as Source Energy.

Who is your "higher self"?

The larger part of us that still exists as Source Energy, this is the Higher Self. This part of ourself exists in the higher spiritual dimensions and is quietly guiding us toward choices and situations that will develop our soul. Which ultimately leads us to a greater understanding of Universal Laws and our own divinity.

The Higher Self does not question our connection to Source and does not doubt our ability to manifest a reality that serves the highest and greatest good to humanity and ourselves. The Higher Self knows that when something is truly satisfying to the soul, it is satisfying to the world.

Why does this matter?

When we learn to embody our Higher Self, here on Earth, we raise the vibration of the entire planet. We step into a sense of self that fulfills us on a soul level. We can feel satisfied in our life's work and feel purposeful. We leave the rat race and are no longer held tightly in the grip of societal standards for happiness and fulfillment.

If you wish to think of this concept in a less spiritual sense, you can think of your Higher Self as the "Best Version of You." See yourself as the person who is thriving in their physical body, living with a pure and kind heart, making time for loved ones, and living true to your greatest good.

How Can I Embody My Higher Self?

1. Understand that this is an ongoing process
2. Meditate
3. Sweat daily
4. Be flexible

5. Recognize your triggers (they are here to help you develop)
6. Stay curious
7. Be open to possibilities
8. Work on your concept of self (your habits, your lifestyle, your likes/dislikes, dietary choices)
9. Spend time alone
10. Spend time in nature

The definition we hold of our Higher Self is can be ever-changing, but it is important that we take the time to define and redefine this definition on a regular basis.

In order to manifest our Higher Self, it is imperative that we put pen to paper and define how our Higher Self looks, thinks, and feels; as well as what the Higher Self accomplishes and in what manner. For this reason, I have included a worksheet on the following pages that can be used for this purpose.

The following questionnaire should be answered from the perspective of your highest and greatest version. For example, if you normally wake up at 8:00 a.m. (but you wish you could wake up at 5:00 a.m.) you would write 5:00 a.m on the line for question one. Or, if you are currently working a job that you do not find fulfilling, you would answer the questionnaire as though you already have your dream career. Writing these affirmations in present tense will signal to universal forces that you are already implementing the changes you wish to make. Doing this will create momentum towards your goals and help you manifest them with greater speed and efficiency.

♦

HIGHER SELF WORKSHEET

1. What time do you wake up?

2. What kinds of foods do you eat?

3. What sort of physical activities do you enjoy daily?

4. How long do you meditate daily?

5. How much water do you drink daily?

6. How many books do you read per month?

7. How often do you see friends and family?

8. What is your career path?

9. How much money do you earn per year? Per month?

10. How do you feel when you wake up in the morning?

11. What time do you go to bed at night?

12. Where do you live?

13. How do you feel when you are at work?

14. What are you grateful for?

HIGHER SELF WORKSHEET

Use the space below to write goals and affirmations that are specific to the life you are trying to create. Use present tense.

_____

_____

_____

_____

_____

_____

_____

_____

_____

_____

_____

A WITCH HAS EARNED HER WISDOM, SHE HAS GONE DEEP WITHIN HER OWN SHADOW AND FOUND THE LIGHT.

SHE STANDS AWARE OF HER POWER.

Chapter Five

CASTING SPELLS

Magic is desire made real.

Often times, when people hear the word "magic" they think of waving wands, gazing into crystal balls, and chanting spells. Images of witches with green faces and pointy black hats circulate in the mind, and a sigh of relief is released as these notions are categorized as the things only of storybooks and Hollywood movies.

The term "spell" has been sensationalized, but the truth is that we are all casting spells daily. The very words we speak and think - these are spells. It is our own volition, intention, and energetic exertion that make spells real, but we do not often ascribe such power to our words (let alone ourselves).

In this book, I will only discuss the topic of casting spells as a focused intention for personal growth or change in the highest and greatest good of the spell-caster. I do not advocate for the usage of spells to bring about change (positive or negative) in the lives of other people. Intentional spell casting is best used as a tool for personal development and spiritual understanding.

LESSON NUMBER ONE IN SPELL CASTING:
Know Your Own Power

We are divine beings. The spark of life that gives us breath is the God force made physical. We are on Earth as spiritual beings living a human experience. Until, as individuals, we can identify the piece of ourselves that is a direct connection to Source Energy, we will never be able to understand our true power. It is because a piece of the Divine lives within our physical bodies as our unique and individual souls, that we have a direct connection to the Divine. Because without the soul, we would not be human, it stands to reason that without the Divine we would not exist. With that understanding, one can make the final conclusion that we, humans, are indeed - the actual physical manifestation of the God Force.

Step one is the beautiful and harrowing process of spiritual investigation that must take place before we can learn to wield this power to make changes in our lives (cast spells). It is the process of going within and discovering that special part of ourselves that is one with the Divine. This could take weeks, or it could take decades; **but we cannot make magic until we understand that we are magicians.**

This process includes a consistent personal spiritual practice and it includes meditation. It includes spending time in nature, exercising the physical body, and feeding it nutritionally dense foods.

Know this: The successful spell-caster is not a victim of his or her own circumstances. The person who casts a spell of intention understands her or his own power and applies it strategically in the form of focus.

LESSON NUMBER TWO IN SPELL CASTING:
Focus

In order to give a spell wings to fly, it needs a power source. That power source is the caster's complete and unwavering focus on the intention of the spell. We must do the spiritual work in order to come to an understanding of our own power, as well as the interworking of natural laws such as vibration and attraction. Only after mastering lesson one, may we move to lesson number two. This is because if we do not truly know we are powerful, it will not be possible to cast a spell with a doubtless mind. Doubt and faithlessness are road blocks to casting spells because without your energetic, mental and emotional focus - the spell does not get off the ground.

If you do not hold these integral beliefs about yourself and the laws of the universe, the results of your spell will be non-existent.

To put it simply: If you do not believe that the results of your spell will manifest, you are energetically blocking the results from manifesting into your life.

Focus is a skill we can learn and strengthen.

In the beginning of your magical journey, it will be necessary to begin using your focus to cast spells with less grandeur. Doing this will enhance your ability to keep steady focus on your goal without expending a great amount of mental or emotional energy.

Ideas for Practice Spells
I will find a coin on the sidewalk today.
I will find a paperclip on the office floor today.
Today I will hear a specific song on the radio.
Today I will see the color yellow everywhere.

We have all noticed coins on the ground and we understand that the world around us is full of color. With this mentality, it does not take much faith or focus to allow these experiences to unfold.

Here is why this works: Casting a spell that you will find a penny today or see the color yellow everywhere does not require a large amount of focus or faith because you may already view these happenings as every-day occurrences.

These small spells also work because you are able to energetically detach from the result, because finding a paperclip isn't going to change your life. The manner in which you hold your intention can make or break your ability to be a successful caster. Seeing if you will actually find a paperclip or penny could be lighthearted and fun, or maybe you forget about it altogether until you find it. This is the best way to hold your magical intentions. Sometimes the things we really want in life, we are actually pushing away because the desire is stale and it doesn't feel good to want it anymore. When your desired intention or spell doesn't feel good in your body, that is when you know it has expired and you need to readjust your energy concerning that particular topic. Keeping it light and fun is essential.

An example of a stale intention is having an enormous desire to lose weight. You have been trying and failing for years to accomplish this desire. Presently, when you think about living more healthfully or weighing less - it just makes you feel discouraged. This example has both elements of an expired desire: You have been wanting it with a great desire for a long period of time and it no longer feels good in your body when you think about it.

A note on stale intentions: Just because your intention is no longer fresh, that does not mean you cannot have the desired result. However, it does mean that you need to energetically disentangle yourself from the desire mixed with frustration and failed attempts. The best way to do this is to remove your focus from that particular goal until you feel energetically 'lighter' towards it.

Once you have practiced these spells and have understood the emotions it takes to conjure the physical manifestation of your thoughts, you will gradually be able to expand your abilities to include the manifestation of things you once thought were beyond the realm of possibility.

I like the exercise of sample spells on page 28 because it can be a practical example of "where our attention goes, energy flows." In doing this, we become more present in the moment as well as strengthen our ability to focus.

Beyond this exercise, I believe that our mental focus can be sharpened by the following:

1. Meditating daily
2. Practicing yoga daily
3. Spending **much** less time in front of digital screens
4. Spending more time in the natural world without headphones
5. Placing our bare feet on the Earth
6. Waking up early enough to witness the sunrise
7. Sleeping an adequate amount of hours nightly

8. Breathing deeply (*Pranayama*)
9. Maintaining a clean and decluttered living space
10. Eating less meat, eggs, and dairy
11. Eating more plant foods
12. Abstaining from alcohol and drugs
13. Staying hydrated with purified water
14. Selecting our sexual partners carefully

LESSON NUMBER THREE IN SPELL CASTING:
Create the Words of Your Spell

The reciting of your words, known as the incantation, is of paramount importance because you are giving voice to your focused intention.

On page 35 of this book, I have shared a few of my own spells to serve as examples or even practice spells for you. When writing the words of your own spells, there are a few elements to remember.

1. Cadence: How you recite the words will make a difference. You will want to speak the words aloud in a sort of poetic notion with inflection and emphasis on important words.

2. Specificity: You can decide to be either specific or general with the words of your spell. The choice is yours, however, you must understand that greater detail requires greater

focus and faith. If you decide to be more general with your wording, you may find that you adopt a greater ability to have faith in the results. For example, a very specific spell will likely include numbers, dates or timelines; where a more general one would include seasons or a range of numbers. **A note on specificity:** It is to your advantage to be as specific as possible, without overstepping your ability to believe in the results.

3. <u>Sonically Pleasing</u>: Allow your words to be artful, poetic, and easy to remember. For proper results, try to present your intention in a way that is short, succinct and memorable. Rhyming is welcomed here, as according to the Wiccan Rede: **"To bind the spell well every time, let the spell be said in rhyme."** Doing so increases the efficacy of your words and it takes more conscious effort to create a rhyme - which translates to a greater energetic payoff.

LESSON NUMBER FOUR IN SPELL CASTING:
Cast Your Spell

If you have done the spiritual work, decided on a topic you wish to enhance in your life, and written the words of your spell - it is time to do the deed. Let's cast!

1. <u>Casting a Circle:</u> When we state our intentions to the Universe, we are opening an energetic portal. When this happens, casting a circle around you will be serving two

purposes: Protection against unwanted outside energy coming into your sacred space, and intensifying your own energy. This circle is an energetic, ethereal boundary. There are many ways to cast a circle, but generally it is done in a clockwise fashion - beginning in the eastern direction. Use your voice to call upon the element of Air (East), the element of Fire (South), the element of Water (West), and finally the element of Earth (North). You may choose to create an actual circle around yourself using the smoke of sage, incense, palo santo, or any other holy wood or herb. You may also decide to make a physical circle around yourself using crystals or other magically consecrated items.

2. <u>Getting Comfortable:</u> Sit in a cross-legged (Padmasana or Lotus Posture) position in the middle of your circle. Allow your mind to settle, and take a few moments to breathe deeply.

3. <u>Speaking Your Spell:</u> Vocalize the beautiful words of your intention. Speak with a voice of confidence, yet reverence to the elemental powers of the Universe.

4. <u>Meditating and Visualizing:</u> This step can actually be practiced throughout the casting, but right after you speak your words it is most powerful. At this point, you are connecting with your Higher Self and communicating your desires. There is absolutely no room for self-doubt, criticism, distractions or general malcontent here. Your true test of focus is in these moments. Meditate on your desired outcome for at least three minutes.

5. <u>Raising Energy:</u> It is time to physically feel your energy adjust to the new status that includes the desired outcome of your spell. Feel inside your energetic body what it would be like to accomplish the desired outcome. Focus all of your own energy, and commune with the elements that we called in during the beginning of the process.

6. <u>Expressing Gratitude:</u> We must show gratitude at the end of a casting for two reasons. The first reason is that we are communing with our Higher Self and the Divine - it is proper to give thanks for their workings on our physical behalf. Second, the vibration of gratitude is one of completion. If we express genuine gratitude for the spell already working, we become a vibrational match to the end result of the spell.

7. <u>Closing the Circle:</u> It is important to finish the process, this indicates that you are moving back into Earthly time and space. To close the circle, walk counter-clockwise thanking each element and direction. Additionally, if you created a physical circle, gather each item one by one while again, speaking words of gratitude.

♦

SPELLS

Higher Self Spell

My body, my heart, my mind, and my soul
I allow my higher-self to take control

I envision my greatest version
And I strive daily to be this person

Decision Making Spell

This or that, which will it be
Many options are available to me

Divine one, help me choose
If you show me the way, I know I cannot lose

Self Love Spell

The spark of the divine dwells within me
With a body to move and eyes to see

I lift my gaze to the Source above
I breathe in the energy of love

SPELL CASTER'S FRIEND

Supplies

1/2 teaspoon cinnamon (for your dreams)
1/2 teaspoon nutmeg (for good luck)
1/2 teaspoon allspice (for healing)
1/2 teaspoon ginger (for the moon)
1/2 teaspoon basil (for protection)
1/2 teaspoon fennel seeds (for spiritual healing)
1/2 teaspoon garlic (for spiritual purification)
1/2 teaspoon marjoram (for extra protection)

Method

Step 1: Place all ingredients in a glass canning jar, close the lid.

Step 2: Shake the jar to mix all of the spices together.

Step 3: Gently remove the lid and inhale the scent before any spell work to increase your power of focus.

Note: Store in a private place and do not reveal the jar to others. This will last for about one year, at which point you should dispose of the contents of the jar by burying it.

GIVE ME MY ROBE, PUT ON MY CROWN; I
HAVE IMMORTAL LONGINGS IN ME.

-WILLIAM SHAKESPEARE
"ANTONY & CLEOPATRA"

Chapter Six

BEAUTY ALCHEMY

O ften times, people scoff at natural remedies and assume they are less effective than cosmeceutical options. However, the recipes I have curated within the next few pages have stood the test of time. Many of these recipes are inspired by beauty routines found around the world for centuries: from the classical Greco-Roman era, to the folk remedies of India, and legendary queens of Ancient Egypt.

You can find references to studies in regards to the efficacy of the ingredients used in the following recipes in the Bibliography section of this book.

In addition, please remember to spot test these mixtures on a small area of your skin before fully applying to make sure you are not allergic to any of the ingredients. I encourage the use of organic ingredients whenever possible.

CLEOPATRA'S FACE MASQUE

Supplies

1 tablespoon bentonite clay
1-4 tablespoons apple cider vinegar (organic + with the mother)
2 teaspoons coffee grounds
small ceramic or glass bowl
wooden spoon or reusable plastic utensil

Method

Step 1: Use a non-metal utensil to place 1 tablespoon of bentonite clay in a small bowl.

Step 2: Place 2 teaspoons of coffee into the bowl.

Step 3: Starting with a small amount, pour the apple cider vinegar into the mixture. Stir until it reaches your preferred consistency.

Step 4: Apply to a clean and dry face.

Step 5: Allow masque to dry, make sure to scrub it off before it dries completely. (20 minutes)

Important Note: When handling this clay, **do not use metal tools like spoons or bowls.** Metal contains positively charged ions, and the clay is saturated with negatively charged ions. Contact with metal will neutralize the ionic charge and render it ineffective. I recommend using the brand **Aztec Secret Indian**

Healing Clay due to the manufacturing process and quality. This brand comes from Death Valley, California, where it is sun-dried for up to six months in temperatures that can reach 134 degrees Fahrenheit.

Ingredient Profile:

Bentonite Clay: For centuries, clays have been used to heal and beautify. Even Cleopatra, Queen of the Nile, used clay from the Nile River and the Arabian desert as part of her beautification rituals over 1800 years ago. Further back still, 4000 years in fact, the spas of ancient Rome featured clay as a tool to calm skin issues and restore youthfulness and vitality to the skin.

Apple Cider Vinegar (ACV): For thousands of years, this vinegar has been used medicinally to treat a variety of ailments from toothaches to dandruff. Cosmetically, ACV has been frequently found in beauty products throughout the ages. Beginning in Roman times, where records show this vinegar being used a toner for the skin. This vinegar is high in malic acid, which is a natural form of alpha-hydroxy-acid. This property makes ACV an extremely effective natural chemical exfoliant.

Coffee Grounds: Organic coffee contains powerful antioxidants such as hydoxycinnamic acids and polyphenols. Hydroxycinnamic acids are very effective at neutralizing free radicals and preventing oxidative stress. Coffee grounds also contain magnesium, which is known as the "relaxation mineral." This mineral is also bioavailable to us transdermally, which means we can absorb it through the skin. In addition, a great benefit of the topical application of coffee comes from the caffeine. When applied to the skin, caffeine fights free radicals (which are responsible for visible signs of aging), soothes inflammation, and tightens the skin. Lastly, the coffee grounds provide an element of physical exfoliation, assisting in the removal of dead skin cells and brightening of the skin.

♦

FREYA'S LUSCIOUS HAIR MASQUE

Supplies

1-5 tablespoons refined and hexane-free castor oil
rosemary essential oil
shower cap
small bowl

Method

Step 1: Depending on the length or your hair, place 1-5 tablespoons of castor oil into a bowl.

Step 2: Add rosemary essential oil into the bowl. I recommend 5 drops per tablespoon of castor oil.

Step 3: Apply this mixture to damp or dry hair (not wet hair).

Step 4: Cover your head with a shower cap or disposable hair processing cap. We cover the head to create a warm environment for the oils. Doing so allows the oils to soak into the scalp, which intensifies their effectiveness.

Step 5: Leave on the head for a minimum of 30 minutes. You can even leave it on overnight.

Step 6: Wash and condition your hair normally to remove the masque.

Ingredient Profile:

Castor Oil: We can trace the use of castor oil for topical remedies all the way back to the ancient Egyptians. During this time in history hair was a symbol of wealth, status, beauty, and fertility (not unlike today). Castor beans have been found in ancient Egyptian tombs dating back to 4000 b.c. Castor oil contains vitamin E, minerals, omega-6 and omega-9 fatty acids. It is also very high in ricinoleic acid, making it beneficial to both skin and hair. This oil contains antibacterial and anti-fungal properties, which helps to dispel folliculitis, dandruff and scalp infections. The ricinoleic acid content increases circulation to the scalp and helps to balance the scalp pH - nourishing existing hair and promoting growth.

Rosemary Essential Oil: This oil improves cellular regeneration. In a randomized comparative trial for the treatment of adrogenetic alopecia, rosemary essential oil performed as well as minoxidil (a common hair growth treatment) with less scalp itching. Historically, the plant is considered sacred by the Egyptians, Hebrews, Greeks, and Romans. These ancient cultures used Rosemary to ward off evil spirits and protect against the plague. Legends of this plant attribute its namesake to the Virgin Mary; she is said to have spread her blue cloak over a rosemary bush as she rested, turning the flowers blue. The shrub became known as the *Rose of Mary*.

◆

HECATE'S HAIR GROWTH MIST

Supplies

2 ounces aloe vera juice

2 ounces purified water

rosemary essential oil

4 oz empty spray bottle

Method:

Step 1: Fill the spray bottle halfway with purified water.

Step 2: Add 10 drops of rosemary essential oil.

Step 3: Fill the remainder of the spray bottle with aloe vera juice. Shake well to combine the ingredients.

Step 4: Spray on wet hair after a shower or dry hair. Style as usual.

Step 5: Store in the refrigerator.

Note: Hecate's Hair Growth Mist is the perfect daily complement to the weekly use of Freya's Luscious Hair Masque on page 42 of this book.

Ingredient Profile:

Aloe Vera: One of the earliest written mentions of the healing benefits of aloe vera dates back to 2100 BCE. The pulp of the aloe vera plant contains 75 active ingredients which include vitamins A, C, E, B12, zinc, and choline. Research has suggested that because aloe vera stimulates blood circulation - it aids in improving the delivery of oxygen and nutrition to the hair follicles, resulting in hair growth.

Rosemary Essential Oil: This oil improves cellular regeneration. In a randomized comparative trial for the treatment of adrogenetic alopecia, rosemary essential oil performed as well as minoxidil (a common hair growth treatment) with less scalp itching. Historically, the plant is considered sacred by the Egyptians, Hebrews, Greeks, and Romans. These ancient cultures used Rosemary to ward off evil spirits and protect against the plague. Legends of this plant attribute its namesake to the Virgin Mary; she is said to have spread her blue cloak over a rosemary bush as she rested, turning the flowers blue. The shrub became known as the *Rose of Mary.*

◆

LAKSHMI'S TEETH WHITENING MAGICK MELTS

Supplies
1/4 cup coconut oil
1 teaspoon ground turmeric
essential oils options (peppermint or spearmint)
ice cube tray

Method:

Step 1: Melt 1/4 cup of coconut oil.

Step 2: Stir in 1 teaspoon of ground turmeric.

Step 3: Add 15-30 drops of the essential oil of your choice.

Step 4: Pour the combined mixture equally into the spaces of an ice cube tray.

Step 5: Store in the refrigerator.

Upon waking, place one of Lakshmi's Teeth Whitening Magick Melts into your mouth, allowing it to melt. Do not swallow. Swish slowly inside your mouth for at least 10 minutes. When you are ready, spit the mixture into the trash. Brush teeth normally.

Ingredient Profile:

Coconut Oil: Traditionally, coconut oil has been used in India as a folk remedy to prevent dental diseases, and strengthen the gums and teeth. In a 2017 randomized controlled study of dental students, the efficacy of coconut oil in controlling levels of plaque was put to the test - and proven to be effective. Subjects rinsed with the oil for 10 minutes, twice per day. The oil also contains high amounts of lauric acid, which has anti-microbial properties.

Tumeric: One study in 2012 found that curcumin (the compound in turmeric that gives the bright yellow color) can prevent gingivitis, assist in removing plaque and bacteria, and reduce inflammation. Most notably for the purposes of this recipe, the bright yellow color does not stain your teeth. In fact, with centuries of use to prove its medicinal powers, turmeric may be beneficial in reducing the appearance of stains on the teeth.

Essential Oils: Choose food-grade essential oils of your choice to enhance the flavor of this recipe.

♦

PERSEPHONE'S LIP SCRUB

Supplies

2 tablespoons coconut sugar
1 teaspoon lemon juice
agave nectar

Method

Step 1: Place 2 tablespoons of coconut sugar into a small bowl.

Step 2: Add 1 teaspoon of lemon juice to the bowl.

Step 3: Slowly stir in drops of agave nectar to the mixture, stopping when desired consistency has been reached. Preferences will vary, you want something sticky enough to grip to the lips.

Step 4: On clean lips, rub the mixture in circular motions. This will remove any dead skin flakes and help to restore a rosy tone to your lips.

Step 5: Lick the remainder of the mixture from your lips or remove with a damp washcloth.

Step 6: Store this mixture in an airtight container. Refrigerate.

Ingredient Profile:

Coconut Sugar: This sugar tastes similar to caramel and is considered **unprocessed and unrefined.** Unlike other types of sugar, this one retains quite a bit of the nutrients found in the coconut palm tree. Minerals like iron, zinc, calcium, and potassium are present in coconut sugar. While these factors set coconut sugar apart, it is still low in overall nutritional value and is not a health food. However, we will be using this ingredient as the physical exfoliant in this recipe. So, no eating required (but certainly not discouraged).

Lemon Juice: The juice of this household yellow citrus fruit contains citric acid, which is a natural bleaching agent. When used on the lips, lemon juice helps to recover the natural pink tone of the lips.

Agave Nectar: This sweetener ranks relatively low on the glycemic index. We are using this sweet liquid as the binding agent of this recipe.

◆

GODDESS BATH RITUAL

Supplies

2 cups epsom salt
1/2 cup bentonite clay mixed into paste
small ceramic or glass bowl
wooden spoon or reusable plastic utensil

Method

Step 1: Place 1/2 cup of bentonite clay in small bowl.

Step 2: Gently pour warm water into the bowl, mixing until a paste forms.

Step 3: Fill your bathtub with water of your desired warmth.

Step 4: Pour 2 cups of epsom salt into the water.

Step 5: Smooth the clay over your body, allowing some to dissolve into the bath water.

Step 6: Soak for at least 25 minutes (minimum amount of time for the minerals to absorb).

Important Note: When handling this clay, do not use metal tools like spoons or bowls. Metal contains positively charged ions, and the clay is saturated with negatively charged ions. Contact with metal will neutralize the ionic charge and render it ineffective. I recommend using the brand **Aztec Secret Indian Healing Clay** due to the manufacturing process and quality. This brand comes from Death Valley, California, where it is sun-dried for up to six months in temperatures that can reach 134 degrees Fahrenheit.

Ingredient Profile:

Epsom Salt: The most important word you need to remember about epsom salt baths is: *Magnesium*. This is such an important mineral and studies suggest that 50% of people in the United States and Europe get less than the daily recommended amount of it. Magnesium, dubbed the "Relaxation Mineral," helps our bodies convert food into energy, helps create and repair DNA, helps to regulate neurotransmitters, and also plays a critical role in mood. Low levels of this mineral are linked to an increased risk of depression. When added to water, epsom salt breaks down into magnesium and sulfate, and magnesium can be absorbed through the skin transdermally.

Bentonite Clay: For centuries, clays have been used to heal and beautify. Even Cleopatra, Queen of the Nile, used clay from the Nile River and the Arabian desert as part of her beautification rituals over 1800 years ago. Further back still, 4000 years in fact, the spas of ancient Rome featured clay as a tool to calm skin issues and restore youthfulness and vitality to the skin.

♦

APHRODITE'S TONER

Supplies

1 rose
5 ounces purified water
boiling tools
rose essential oil (optional)
4 oz spray bottle

Method

Step 1: Bring 5 ounces of water to a boil

Step 2: Add the petals of at least 1 rose to the water.

Step 3: Simmer the roses for about 10 minutes.

Step 4: After allowing adequate cooling time, strain the roses and pour the water into the bottle.

Step 5: Use as a facial or full body toner on clean skin by applying to skin after a shower or bath. Apply before any additional products are applied. You can also add the leftover petals to a bath if you would like.

Important Note: For this toner, I recommend using red rose petals, because they are the highest vibrational flower. However, please feel free to use any color of rose you feel drawn to. I also recommend finding roses that have not been sprayed with unnatural chemicals for preserve freshness or color.

Ingredient Profile:

Rose Petals: When boiled in water, the essence of the rose petals will become one with the water - forming **rosewater**. One of the greatest benefits of rose water is its strong anti-inflammatory properties. When applied to the skin, it may even help soothe irritation caused by eczema, rosacea, and acne. Historically, the rose flower is an attribute to Venus, the Roman goddess of love and beauty (Aphrodite in Greece). The Damask Rose was originally discovered in Persia; ancient tales tell of Persian princesses filling the palace fountains with rose water so that drops would land upon their skin like light rain fall.

Rose Essential Oil: This ingredient is optional, but can add extra intensity to the toning mist. The roses used to prepare rose essential oil are usually cultivated in Iran, and because roses are not by nature an oily plant, large amounts of the petals are needed in order to produce a significant amount of the oil. This means that that pure oil of rose is one of the most precious and expensive in the world. Culturally, this flower has been cherished for centuries. According to traditional Chinese medicine, rose promotes the movement of Qi (life force energy) within the body. In ancient Persian culture (present day Iran) they speak of the rose as being supernatural with the saying, "The rose is the only thing you can take with you when die, because it is not of this world."

♦

LET FOOD BE THY MEDICINE, AND MEDICINE
BE THY FOOD.

-HIPPOCRATES

Chapter Seven

KITCHEN ALCHEMY

We become an alchemist in the kitchen when we combine common ingredients and make them taste delicious! By preparing ordinary ingredients with love, we treat our bodies with the respect and nutrition they deserve. We all have the power to transform into our greatest versions.

What we feed our body has a direct impact on how we feel, how we look, and how we manage stress. When I began eating a healthy and balanced plant-based diet, my body responded extremely well. This is when I started making the connection between what I eat and how I feel.

Since switching to a vegan diet in 2014, I have noticed:

Clearer Skin: I get fewer breakouts and my skin is generally less reactive and bumpy.

Longer and Shiner Hair: Plant foods offer an abundance of micronutrients that are nourishing to the hair.

Less Food Guilt: Food guilt is when you feel badly or guilty after you eat because you know the food did not provide optimal nutrition. You know you could have made better choices, and you feel guilty for not doing so.

Weight Maintenance: I am able to stay at the optimal weight for my body, while eating large portions of delicious foods.

Increased Energy: Eating the bodies of animals and animal byproducts is taxing on the human digestive system. When I used to eat animal products at every meal, it would result in feelings of lethargy and demotivation. My body was using a large amount of energy to digest the meat, eggs, and dairy which resulted in less energy for the activities I enjoy.

More Restful Sleep: Plant foods are rich in micronutrients, vitamins, and minerals. When we cut out animal products and add in large quantities of plants, our bodies receive the nutrition needed to operate properly. When all of our nutritional storehouses are filled up, not only does the body operate properly during waking hours - but during sleep as well.

◆

BANANA ICE CREAM (FOUR WAYS)

BLUEBERRY VANILLA ICE CREAM

Supplies

1 frozen banana
1/2 cup frozen wild blueberries
1/2 cup vanilla soy milk
1 scoop vegan vanilla protein powder
1 handful of spinach (optional)

Note: A high-powered blender such as a Vitamix is recommended (but not required) for best result. Each recipe can be enjoyed as one serving. **I highly recommend waiting until bananas are very ripe and spotted before freezing them.**

Method

Step 1: Place all ingredients into your Vitamix.
Step 2: Blend on low, slowly increasing speed for 60 seconds.
Step 3: Transfer to a bowl to enjoy immediately.
Note: Store any leftovers in freezer.

Health Benefits:

♦Bananas are one of the best fruit sources of vitamin B6.
♦Wild blueberries are richer in antioxidants than farmed ones.
♦Blueberries are the most nutrient dense berries, and the Queen of antioxidant foods.
♦Blueberries reduce DNA damage, which protects against aging.

CHOCOLATE BANANA ICE CREAM

Supplies

2 frozen bananas

1/2 cup vanilla soy milk

1 scoop vegan chocolate protein powder

1 handful of spinach (optional)

Method

Step 1: Place all ingredients into your Vitamix,

Step 2: Blend on low, slowly increasing speed for 60 seconds.

Step 3: Transfer to a bowl to enjoy immediately.

Note: Store any leftovers in freezer, I encourage the use of organic ingredients whenever possible.

Health Benefits:

♦One banana contains 13% of the daily value of manganese, helping the body make collagen.

♦Using plant-based protein powder is a smarter option because whey protein will contribute to the formation of Ama in the body *(pg. 12)*.

MINT CHOCOLATE ICE CREAM

Supplies

2 frozen bananas

1/2 cup vanilla soy milk

5-10 fresh mint leaves

1 scoop vegan chocolate protein powder

Method

Step 1: Place all ingredients into your Vitamix.

Step 2: Blend on low, slowly increasing speed for 60 seconds.

Step 3: Transfer to bowl to enjoy immediately.

Note: Store any leftovers in freezer, I encourage the use of organic ingredients whenever possible.

Health Benefits:

♦The potassium in bananas is vital for heart health, especially blood pressure control.

♦Mint leaves have been shown to help aid indigestion and upset stomach.

STRAWBERRY BANANA ICE CREAM

Supplies

1 frozen banana
1/2 cup vanilla soy milk
1 cup frozen strawberries
1 scoop vanilla protein powder

Method

Step 1: Place all of the ingredients into your Vitamix.

Step 2: Blend on low, slowly increasing speed for 60 seconds.

Step 3: Transfer to a bowl and enjoy immediately.

Note: Store any leftovers in freezer, I encourage the use of organic ingredients whenever possible.

Health Benefits:

♦Bananas contain many potent antioxidants such as catechins and dopamine. Although, in this form dopamine is not a mood enhancer, it simply acts as a strong antioxidant.

♦Strawberries are abundant in anthocyanin, folate, manganese, and vitamin C.

PUMPKIN SEED MILK

Supplies

1 cup soaked pumpkin seeds
3 cups purified water
pinch of pink Himalayan salt

Method

Step 1: Overnight, soak pumpkin seeds in just enough water to cover them.

Step 2: Strain pumpkin seeds and discard the water used for soaking.

Step 3: Add ingredient list to your blender.

Step 4: Pulse blender for about 60 seconds, some seed pulp will remain.

Step 5: Strain milk into a canning jar.

Step 6: Use on cereal, in coffee, in smoothies, etc.

Step 7: Store in the refrigerator for up to 5 days in a canning jar with lid tightly closed.

Note: Use the pumpkin seed pulp to make the granola recipe on the next page. I encourage the use of organic ingredients whenever possible.

Health Benefits:

♦Pumpkin seeds contain high amounts of zinc.

♦The body does not naturally produce zinc, so we must get it through foods.

♦Zinc is required for proper immune function and protein synthesis within the body.

PUMPKIN SEED GRANOLA

Supplies

1 teaspoon cinnamon

1 teaspoon vanilla extract

pinch of pink Himalayan salt

leftover pulp from making the pumpkin seed milk recipe pg. 62

parchment paper and baking sheet

Method

Step 1: Save the pumpkin seed pulp from previous recipe.

Step 2: Preheat your oven to 325 degrees.

Step 3: Place all ingredients into a small bowl and combine.

Step 4: Place parchment paper on baking sheet.

Step 5: Spread the mixture evenly onto the baking sheet.

Step 6: Bake for 25 minutes, checking halfway through to see if granola needs to be rotated.

Step 7: Use as topping for banana ice cream, smoothie bowls, vegan yogurt, etc.

Step 8: Store in an airtight container, no need to refrigerate.

Health Benefits:

♦Pumpkin seeds contain high amounts of iron, magnesium, and other minerals.

♦Only a small amount of seeds is needed to get the nutritional benefits (one ounce).

♦Pink Himalayan salt is extracted from the Khewra Salt Mine in Pakistan, which is one of the oldest salt mines in the world. This type of salt contains more minerals than table salt.

DESIGN YOUR OWN SMOOTHIE

Choose 1 Liquid

1 cup oat milk

1 cup soy milk

1 cup almond milk

1 cup coconut water

1 cup purified water

1 cup fruit juice

Choose 2 Fruits + Vegetables

2 stalks of celery

1 apple

1 cup blueberries

1 cup pineapple

1 cup grapes

1 cup strawberries

1 carrot

1 banana

Choose 1 Green

1 romaine heart

2 cups spinach

1 small head of Boston lettuce

1 cup kale

Method

Step 1: Add to blender, slowly increase speed for 60 seconds.

Step 2: Add 1 cup of ice for a thicker texture.

VEGAN CHOCOLATE MUG CAKE

Supplies

2.5 tablespoons oat flour

1.5 tablespoons cacao powder

2 tablespoons coconut sugar

1/4 teaspoon baking powder

pinch of pink Himalayan salt

1 tablespoon melted coconut oil

3 tablespoons non-dairy milk

1/2 teaspoon pure vanilla extract

Method

Step 1: Add the flour, cacao powder, sugar and baking powder to a mug. Stir to combine.

Step 2: Stir the oil, non-dairy milk and vanilla into the mug.

Step 3: Cook in the microwave for 60 seconds.

Health Benefits:

♦This mug cake is a delicious and fun treat that warms the soul and satisfies chocolate cravings.

♦Cacao is generally considered to be native to the Mayan civilization of Central America, it is used in ritual ceremonies around the time of the new moon. During this time in history, cacao was considered so sacred that it was only consumed ritualistically.

♦Cacao is rich in the naturally occurring antioxidant group called *polyphenols*, which are known for their anti-inflammatory effects.

BASIL LEMONADE

Supplies

3 cups purified water
1.5 lemons (peeled, cut in half with seeds removed)
1/4 cup sweetener of choice (sugar, date syrup, etc.)
1/3 cup fresh basil leaves
1 cup ice cubes

Method

Step 1: Place all ingredients in a large blender.
Step 2: Blend for 60 seconds, gradually increasing speed.
Step 2: Store in a glass container in the refrigerator.

Health Benefits:

♦Lemons are high in vitamin C and soluble fiber. By adding the entire lemon (with pulp) to this beverage, we are optimizing the amount of fiber intake.

♦Lemons help prevent anemia by improving the body's ability to absorb iron.

♦Basil is a member of the mint family and originates in Asia and Africa. The type of basil commonly used in teas is called *Tulsi* or *Holy Basil.* In Hindu culture, this herb is associated with Lakshmi, the goddess of beauty, love, and abundance. Ayurvedic medicine holds this herb in high regard calling it *the herb that nourishes the spirit.*

♦Basil reduces the circulation of stress hormones in the body.

YOGA IS THE JOURNEY OF THE SELF, THROUGH
THE SELF, TO THE SELF.

-THE BHAGAVAD GITA

Chapter Eight

YOGA

The practice of yoga is less about stretching and flexibility than our modern world would have you believing. Yoga is less about doing complicated balancing poses, and more about the days we show up to our mats even when we do not feel like doing so. This practice is about understanding the flow of energy within the body, and how to work **with** our bodies instead of against them.

Through yoga, we offer ourselves a truly invaluable insight into where we might be holding ourselves back in life. We can feel into our bodies as we flow through the asanas and see where the energy is stagnant. We can measure our progress by noticing how much more open we feel - physically, mentally, and emotionally.

Mental anguish, stress, sadness, depression, anxiety, emotional trauma, mental abuse, negative self-talk (and much more) can take on a physical presence in the body in the form of muscle tightness, muscle knots, and joint issues. When we do not properly express, work through and transmute these emotions the body's only method of allowing you to live your daily life is to store them.

This temporary emotional storage solution might get you through your day-to-day life, if you do not eventually unpack them, it is going to cause serious health issues down the road. These emotions can show up as life-altering and unmanageable cases of depression, anxiety, lack of ambition, or another chronic mental health conditions. It can also show up as physical dis-eases in the body such as psoriasis, acne, hair loss, gastro-intestinal issues, chronic fatigue, and cancer.

This is why some people may experience a release of emotions during a yoga class characterized by a sudden urge to physically express the emotions through crying or laughing for no seen reason. An emotional release can also come in the form of sudden emotions overtaking your consciousness such as a sudden surge of extreme anger, euphoria or sadness. t is important to remember that these emotions are bubbling to the surface (finally!) and it is okay to feel them and allow them to be released. Yoga gives us the gift of being able to unpack our hidden emotional suitcase in order to live a more peaceful life.

"Do not dwell in the past, do not dream of the future. Concentrate only on the present moment."

— Guatama Buddha

Over time, certain body parts have been linked to certain emotions. Although not absolute, the list below can help you identify why you may have tightness in certain areas of the body.

EMOTIONAL STORAGE SYSTEM

Neck: Stubbornness, not wanting to see alternatives, rigidity in decision making, obsessive need to be right all the time, not seeing the value in constructive criticism, taking on too many responsibilities

Shoulders: A generally negative outlook on life can feel like the 'weight of the world is on your shoulders,' constantly wanting what you do not have and not appreciating where you are in life, lack of gratefulness

Upper Back: Loneliness, abandonment, feeling unloved, feeling undesirable, withdrawing our own love

Mid-Back: Ruminating on the past, not letting go of the past, not seeing a bright future, guilt, thinking your best days are behind you, "the grass is greener on the other side" mentality, insomnia

Lower Back: A constant mentality of financial scarcity, operating on a subconscious fear of abundance, money issues, pay check to pay check mentality, anger

Elbows: Inability to change the course of your life in a positive way, fear of new experiences, lack of ability to see change in a positive light, fear of change

Wrists: Lack of flow in life, constant need for structure with no room for fluidity

Hips: Fear of making big decisions, lack of goal setting and inability to see the future as kind, fear of what is to come, fear of the future

Knees: Inability to bend the rules and routines you set for yourself, tendency to act out of pride, obsession with rule-following and routines

Ankles: Fear of receiving pleasure, guilt regarding pleasure

Feet: Fear of the future and not stepping forward in life

Heart and Chest: Emotional hurt, not properly mourning the ending of relationships, the pain of heart-break from past relationships.

Headaches: Needing to control everything, inability to surrender to the flow of life

Stomach: Fear of unwanted outcomes, general feelings of fear

Throat: Inability to speak up for the self, stifled anger or creativity, holding in words of anger, inability to express the true self

THE EIGHT LIMBS OF YOGA

The practice of yoga extends far beyond what we do on our yoga mats, and yet what we do on our yoga mat can be the perfect illustration of the Eight Limbs of Yoga.

<u>The Eight Limbs of Yoga</u>
Yamas - Ethical Disciplines
Niyamas - Self Observation
Asana - Posture
Pranayama - Breath Control
Pratyahara - Sense Withdrawal
Dharana - Concentration
Dhyana - Meditation
Samadhi - A State of Joy

When most people think of yoga today, we think primarily of the third limb: *Asana*. Downward dog is an asana, tree pose is an asana, and warrior two is an asana. Even the Sanskrit words for these postures contain the suffix "asana. "

Downward Dog - Adho Mukha Svanasana
Tree Pose - Vrikasana
Warrior Two - Virabhadrasana II

Some may think of the final resting pose of a yoga class, *Savasana*, and relate it to the seventh limb of *Dhyana* or meditation. This would all be correct, and yet there is more to know. Yoga is a lifestyle, a way of being, and a state of existence in the world. Yoga is a presence in the mind, body, and spirit.

In fact, the word "Yoga" means "Union" - and we seek to connect to these three aspects of the self through a yoga practice. Through concentration on the Eight Limbs of Yoga, we can begin to unify these three aspects within ourselves. When practiced regularly, we nourish ourselves in a way that brings about positive physical, mental, and emotional change.

Patanjali, the author of the Yoga Sutras, describes the Eight Limbs of Yoga as the limbs of a tree. Self-awareness, wisdom and the development of a spiritual practice grow and unfold slowly - much like the limbs of a tree. These fruits of life come from nourishing our bodies, watering ourselves with wisdom, and being patient while allowing time to teach us. We cannot expect to suddenly go from a seed to a beautiful and tall apple tree with ripe fruit on every branch. Consistently practicing the Eight Limbs over an extended period of time will lead to spiritual insights, self-actualization, and a more connected way of living.

It is through our daily practices and habits that we grow into the best versions of ourselves. Only through consistency of habit (taking the correct action), consistency of mind (monitoring our thoughts), and consistency of emotion (learning to balance our inner world) may we taste the fruit of the tree. If we want to experience a state of true joy, bliss or *Samadhi* - we have the responsibility of making the other seven of the limbs a priority in our busy lives.

<u>Yamas and Niyamas:</u> At first, personal insights begin manifesting into our conscious awareness. We notice ourselves choosing certain foods while avoiding others. We may begin being more truthful with our words, and choosing our words more carefully. An urge for self-study and inner exploration may emerge. At this point we are stepping into the first two limbs, which can be boiled down to "Yoga Ethics."

The Five Yamas
Ahimsa - Non-violence
Satya - Truthfulness
Asteya - Non-stealing
Brahmacharya - Non-excess
Aparigraha - Non-greed

The Five Niyamas
Saucha - Purity
Santosha - Contentment
Tapas - Training your physical senses, self-discipline
Svadhyaya - Inner exploration, self-study
Ishvara Pranidhana - Surrender

I want to make specific mention of *Ahimsa* to point out that this is the reason many yogis adopt a vegan diet and lifestyle. Some believe that abstaining from animal products of all kinds (foods, and textiles like leather or wool) to be an integral part of spiritual awakening. While it does, indeed, create a healthier physical body and contribute to the success of *Saucha*, it is the mentality behind this decision that brings about the most change.

The decision to stop treating animals as a commodity to be separated from their families, killed, processed, packaged, bought and sold is a sign the evolution of our species. Ethical vegans believe that the character of a civilization should be judged by how the most helpless and voiceless members are treated. And in our case, farmed, caged, and hunted animals are the most helpless. These animals are so voiceless that most humans believe the voice to be nonexistent.

<u>Asana and Pranayama:</u> We grow the next two limbs by practicing conscious breathing exercises as discussed in chapter nine of this book. During a traditional yoga class, focus should be applied to the breath, making sure it is smooth and balanced while flowing in and out through the nostrils. If the difficulty of an asana is challenging and this causes our breath to become labored, the proper practice is to modify the asana until breathing can be stabilized. In this way, one can see how these two limbs are intertwined.

<u>Pratyahara:</u> While keeping the mind intently focused on the quality of the breath, monitoring it at all times, the senses begin to turn inward. Our inner world becomes our primary focus, and thus the physical senses withdraw.

<u>Dharana:</u> The conscious awareness that our concentration has moved from the breath to something external like the clock or other yoga students in the class is the first step in developing Dharana. As we improve our ability to control the mind and keep it from wandering, concentration deepens and it is at this

point we are practicing this limb successfully. Developing control of our own mind is the essence of Dharana.

Dhyana: We can manifest Dhyana, or a meditative state, by going deeper into the concentration we learn to cultivate during Dharana. An extra layer of refinement occurs and our ability to remain in the present is greatly enhanced.

Samadhi: A meditative mind is fertile soil for achieving the state of joy that exists as we realize that we are one with the Divine. Perfect union is realized. We understand that our individualized soul is one with Infinite Spirit. See the 7th stage of spiritual alchemy on page 17 of this book for another spiritual perspective of this process.

◆

SURYA NAMASKAR

I invite you to try the following yoga sequence daily, as one of your first priorities upon waking. The following sequence is universally recognized as Suyra Namaskar or *Sun Salutation*. You can think of this as a way to connect to Source Energy and your Higher Self.

This twelve-fold classic sequence is performed as reverence to the solar deity, the words below can be chanted out loud or silently in the mind during this sequence.

Om Ravaye Namah - to the radiant one,
Om Suryaya Namaha - to the dispeller of darkness,
Om Pooshne Namaha - to the universal nourisher,
Om Khagaya Namah - to the all-pervading one.

Moving the body through this selection of asanas (yoga poses), we begin to ignite the energy of the sun within our physical bodies. We notice evidence of our inner solar energy as we feel the heat rising within us, our bodies beginning to perspire, and the light in our eyes brightening.

The first time through the Surya Namaskar sequence, you will lead with the left leg. The second time through the 12 postures, you will lead with the right leg. In total, one full round of Sun Salutation is 24 steps. After one full round, you may begin at the first posture and lead with the left leg again, then switch legs. Depending on which tradition of yoga is best for you, you may decide to complete anywhere from 3 to 20 rounds total.

SURYA NAMASKAR SEQUENCE

1. <u>Pranamasana:</u> Bring your hands together in the middle of the chest, forming Anjali Mudra (prayer hands). Take a moment to center your energy and breathe deeply.

2. <u>Hasta Uttanasana:</u> When you are ready, inhale through the nose as you lift your hands overhead. You can keep the hands in Anjali Mudra or switch to Kali Mudra (*pictured in figure 2*).

3. <u>Uttanasana:</u> On your next exhale, fold forward. Bring your palms to touch the floor and do not lock your knees.

4. <u>Anjaneyasana:</u> Inhale as you step your left leg back as far as possible. Drop the knee and untuck the toes. You may rest your hands on your knee or place the palms on the mat.

5. <u>Dandasana:</u> Retain the inhale as you step the right leg back to meet the left.

6. <u>Kitakasana:</u> Exhale as you lower your chest to the mat while keeping the hips high.

7. <u>Bhujangasana:</u> Inhale while lifting your head and neck, arch your back and untuck the toes. Keep the shoulders relaxed and open the chest area.

8. <u>Adho Mukha Svanasana:</u> Exhale while you curl the toes under and push the hips up and back. Spread your fingers wide on the mat and gaze between your legs.

9. <u>Anjaneyasana:</u> Inhale while stepping forward with the left leg, placing it between the hands. Drop your knee to the floor and untuck the toes.

10. <u>Uttanasana:</u> Exhale, stepping forward to bring both feet together at the top of the mat. Palms should be as close to the floor as possible.

11. <u>Hasta Uttanasana:</u> Inhale, sweeping the arms overhead. Stretch the arms up and back while hands are in either Kali or Anjali Mudra.

12. <u>Pranamasana:</u> Take your final exhale, bringing the hands back to heart center. Straighten your body to standing position. Take a moment to relax here. Prepare to move through the sequence a second time, starting with the opposite leg this time.

♦

The inhale and exhale pattern is an integral aspect of this sequence. You will notice that any of the expansive movements will be paired with an inhale, while the folding and constricting movements are paired with an exhale. Performing the asanas in this way provides the maximum benefits of these postures.

1. Pranamasana (Prayer)

2. Hasta Uttanasana
(Arms Raised)

3. Uttanasana (Forward Fold)

4. Anjaneyasana (Low Lunge)

5. Dandasana (Plank)

6. Kitakasana (Worm)

7. Bhujangasana (Cobra)

8. Adho Mukha Svanasana
(Downward Facing Dog)

9. Anjaneyasana (Low Lunge)

10. Uttanasana (Forward Fold)

11. Hasta Uttanasana
(Arms Raised)

12. Pranamasana (Prayer)

TIPS FOR A STRONGER YOGA PRACTICE

Drishti: Keeping your eyes softly focused on a particular spot in front of you is called *Drishti*. This focused gaze assists with balancing postures and it helps to calm mental chatter. Different asanas may call for differing focal points. For example, gazing down at a particular spot on the floor will be more grounding, calming, and centering. Taking your gaze upward will cultivate a sense of openness and energetic flow.

Breath: Steady breathing is the most important element of a yoga practice. If your breathing becomes shallow and from the chest, this is a sign that your endurance is not built up yet. While practicing yoga, the breath should always come through the nostrils (no mouth breathing) and go deep into the belly. The breath is our link to life force energy, or *Prana*, so it is important that we take it seriously. This being said, at certain times during the practice, it is permissible and beneficial to take an exhale through the mouth. This is called a *cleansing breath*. It can be done a handful of times throughout an hour long practice. Be aware that letting energy out through the mouth gives away our precious energy - so only do this when you are consciously releasing a thought pattern.

Mind Set: We should always take the time to set an intention at the beginning of our yoga practice. You will be creating energy with the movements of your body, and this energy can be directed with the mind. Choose to offer your practice to a deity, to your goals, or to a loved one. Reviewing the Higher Self Worksheet on page 23 may help you set a focused intention.

INHALE, AND GOD APPROACHES YOU.

HOLD THE INHALATION, AND GOD REMAINS IN YOU.

EXHALE, AND YOU APPROACH GOD.

HOLD THE EXHALATION, AND YOU SURRENDER TO GOD.

-KRISHNAMACHARYA

Chapter Nine

PRANAYAMA

The word "Pranayama" is a Sanskrit word meaning "breath restraint." We can explore this further, knowing that restraint in this context means *control*. We can find mention of this ancient practice within the 8 Limbs of Yoga – Pranayama is the 4th limb.

Breathing properly is the main goal of a yoga practice. Allowing the lower belly, chest and back, and clavicle areas to fill up with breath is an utterly fantastic way to bring fresh energy into the body. Similarly, allowing total exhalation from these areas is an excellent way to dispel negative or stagnant energy. You can see how engaging in breathing exercises would be beneficial in purifying a person's physical body and energetic field.

Our external beauty can also be enhanced through a regular breath-work practice. Pranayama oxygenates the physical body, resulting in a healthy glow that cannot be bought with cosmetics.

The practice of Pranayama can involve holding the breath, engaging in controlled yogic exhales or inhales, utilizing alternate nostril breathing, inhaling passively after a forceful exhale, etc. These (and more) are all ways we can begin to introduce breath restraint, or *Pranayama,* into daily life.

Along with breathing exercises, we practice the formation of hand gestures, known as *Mudras.* The universe is comprised of five basic elements and our fingers are representative of each one. Through the fingers, we are constantly emitting vital life-force energy and electric waves. Yogis believe that when we join specific fingers together in the form of Mudras, an electro-electro-magnetic current begins. This action stimulates our consciousness while promoting health and creating balance and harmony within our physical, mental and emotional bodies.

Thumb - Fire (Agni)
Index Finger - Air (Vayu)
Middle Finger - Space (Akash)
Ring Finger - Earth (Prithvi)
Little Finger - Water (Jal)

KAPALABHATI

This style of breath work is invigorating and warming. It helps to cleanse the lungs, sinuses, and respiratory system – which can help to prevent illness and allergies. Regular practice of this technique will strengthen the diaphragm and abdominal muscles. This exercise also increases your body's oxygen supply, which stimulates and energizes the brain while preparing it for meditation and work that requires high focus.

Method

Step 1: Sit up straight in a cross-legged position.

Step 2: Place your hands, palms up, on your knees.

Step 3: Bring the thumb and pointer fingers together, forming what looks like the OK symbol. This hand position is known as *Chin Mudra.*

Step 4: Through the nose, begin taking full breaths into the belly. The lower belly should expand fully with each slow inhale. Repeat as many times as you feel necessary.

Step 5: When you are ready, begin to exhale through the nose with short forceful breaths, contracting the abdominal muscles.

Note: When done correctly, this sort of exhale should result in an automatic, or *passive*, inhale.

Step 6: Repeat this breathing pattern for 20-40 repetitions.

Step 7: After the final forceful exhale, breathe deeply into the belly and hold for 20 seconds.

Step 8: Slowly exhale.

♦

ANULOMA-VILOMA

This variation of Pranayama is also known as alternate nostril breathing. It is considered the best technique to handle stress, anxiety, and other mental pressures. Regular practice improves blood circulation, making a positive impact on the heart. It also helps to reduce snoring. Anuloma-Viloma clears blocked energy channels in the body and promotes feelings of balance and harmony.

Method

Step 1: Sit up straight in a cross-legged position.

Step 2: Place your hands, palms up, on your knees.

Step 3: With your left hand, bring the thumb and pointer fingers together, forming what looks like the OK symbol, this hand position is known as *Chin Mudra*. Holding this mudra, gently rest this hand back on your knee.

Step 4: The right hand will form *Vishnu Mudra* by curling the pointer and middle finger into the palm. The right hand will hold this mudra throughout the breathing exercise while actively holding the nostrils.

Step 5: Inhale through both nostrils, use the thumb of the right hand to close the right nostril and exhale through the left nostril.

Step 6: Keeping the right nostril closed, inhale through only the left side and hold for 5 counts.

Step 7: Use the ring finger of the right hand to close the left nostril. Hold the breath for a count of 20.

Step 8: Keeping the left side closed, exhale the breath using the right nostril only to a count of 10.

Step 9: Keep the left side closed and inhale only the right side to a count of 5.

Step 10: Use the thumb of the right hand to close the right nostril. Hold the breath for a count of 20.

Step 11: Keep the right nostril closed and exhale through the left nostril only for a count of 10.

Step 12: This completes one round of *Anuloma-Viloma*. Repeat steps 5-12, three more times.

◆

THE SECRET TO CHANGE IS TO FOCUS ALL OF YOUR ENERGY, NOT ON FIGHTING THE OLD, BUT ON BUILDING THE NEW.

-SOCRATES

Chapter Ten

CREATING YOUR HOME SANCTUARY

Your home can be your sacred refuge. Whether you work from home, live with roommates, have a small or large area to work with - you can still implement one or many of the following inspirations to create beautiful surroundings. Building a spiritual nest might seem like something only available to a "certain type of person" and maybe you have reservations about seeing yourself in that light. The truth is that we can all benefit from putting a bit more effort into our surroundings.

Our homes should be set up for our continued growth and success. We should take the time to cultivate a space that inspires us to achieve our spiritual and wellness goals. In many cultures, the home is considered an extension of the soul itself.

HOW TO GET STARTED

1. <u>Declutter your space</u>: When deciding to keep an item, as yourself: Is it functional and do you actually use it? Does it hold a special meaning? Does it create a feeling of joy in your heart? Consider donating or selling items that do not meet these criteria. Keeping extraneous and unused items can create a stressful and uneasy environment. In the ancient practice of Feng Shui, it is known that decluttering can increase the chi (life force) energy in your home by allowing energy to flow freely and circulate.

2. <u>Bring the outdoors in:</u>

    Plants: Bright flowers and house plants can add vibrancy to your space. During the late 1980's, NASA began studying houseplants in order to provide cleaner air for space stations. They learned that there are many houseplants that can help to purify the air by filtering out harmful compounds in the air. The following plants have been proven to purify air: Peace Lily (number one on NASA's list), Snake Plant, Bamboo Palm, Money Bonsai, Rubber Plant, and Aloe Vera. In addition, scientific research shows that house plants boost our mood, creativity, and productivity. **Note**: If you have pets, please check to see if any plant you bring home could be poisonous to them.

    Wood: Bringing natural materials and textures, such as genuine wood, into your home helps to mimic the natural world. Spending all day at an office full of computers and harsh lighting can be jarring to the body. Hardwood flooring, exposed wooden ceiling beams, or natural wood decor items can help to steady the mind and bring a sense of calm.

Stones (crystals, granite): We can choose to include certain design elements in our homes for not only aesthetic purposes, but functionality. Using granite or quartz for countertops is efficient, beautiful, and also brings the outdoors in. Having contact with the natural materials daily while cooking or doing our nightly skincare routine helps to ground our energy. These natural materials are forged from the Earth and carry the vibration of the Earth; our bodies recognize this and are naturally soothed by the presence of these materials.

Crystals work in a similar way, but they carry a unique and specific energy based on their molecular properties. Shamans and healers have known about these properties for millennia; these special "pretty rocks" have been incorporated into spiritual practices throughout history and found in holy texts and at archaeological sites. Subtle energies (vibration) underlies all of physical reality and forms the basis of matter. This is true of living things, like humans and animals; it is also true of perceived inanimate objects such as crystals.

Even if that vibration is not readily detectable by our five senses, science shows that the vibration exists. Not only does it exist, but each individual holds a unique vibrational signature. If we take the time to study the individual properties of crystals, we can begin to understand which ones may be most suitable for our own homes. I have included a guide that may help you discover with which crystals you may resonate.

CRYSTAL REFERENCE GUIDE

Space Cleansing: Black Tourmaline, Clear Quartz

Centering: Blue Lace Agate, Clear Quartz

Relieving Anxiety and Stress: Lapis Lazuli, Blue Lace Agate, Black Tourmaline, Blue Kyanite

Releasing Anger: Carnelian, Amber, Black Tourmaline

Healing Addictions: Labradorite, Amethyst

Allowing Abundance and Prosperity: Citrine, Garnet, Aventurine

Enhancing Willpower and Self-Worth: Onyx, Citrine, Hematite

Fostering Healthy Relationships: Rose Quartz, Lapis Lazuli, Yellow Tigers Eye

Protection: Black Tourmaline, Amethyst

Increasing Positive Energy: Clear Quartz, Smoky Quartz

Igniting Passion: Pink Tourmaline, Pyrite, Garnet

Healing Obsessions and Compulsions: Citrine, Amethyst, Ametrine, Herkimer Diamond

Sparking Motivation and Dispelling Laziness: Carnelian, Rainbow Fluorite, Calcite

Regulating Mood Swings: Smoky Quartz, Sodalite

Dispelling Loneliness: Rose Quartz, Rutilated Quartz

Decreasing Irritability: Green Jade, Peridot

Enhancing Intuition: Celestite, Amethyst

Dispelling Insomnia: Moonstone, Amethyst

Grounding: Obsidian, Black Tourmaline, Lodestone

Enhancing Faith: Moonstone, Labradorite, Selenite

Balancing Emotions: Garnet, Malachite, Rainbow Fluorite

Fire: Another way we can bring the outdoors into our home is through the use of the element of fire. Of course, we want to do this in a controlled way by using candles and fireplaces. Fire is represented in alchemy by the sun and its light. Fire is also the element of transformation. It has esoteric associations with stamina, strength, vitality, creativity, and enlightenment. When we consciously bring the element of fire into our sacred space, we are inviting those same qualities into our energetic field. We can also use candles as a meditation tool, gazing into the flame and allowing a hypnotic state to alter our consciousness. Dimmable lamps, candles, fireplaces, and design elements of red can all stimulate the qualities of fire.

Water: Add flow to your sanctuary by incorporating the element of water. Bubbling fountains and fish tanks will do the trick. In Feng Shui, mirrors are also associated with the water element due to their reflective quality. Water stimulates feelings of peace and calm, as it subconsciously takes us back to our first memories of existence within the womb. This element helps us to tap into that innate sense of tranquility. You may also choose to incorporate images of water or beaches throughout your home or decorate with blue glass.

Air: Making sure the air is always fresh in your sanctuary is very important for many reasons. In Feng Shui, the element of air represents mental logic and intellectual abilities. It is also the element that invites a sense of open-mindedness, artistry, and humanitarianism. To enhance these qualities in yourself, try to incorporate the element of air into your surroundings. Air should circulate freely, without stagnation. Placing fans in your home, as well as opening windows is an obvious way to cultivate this healthy air-flow. You may also choose to diffuse essential oils, light incense, smudge the air with sage or palo santo, play soothing music, or purchase an a HEPA air filter. Any or all of these choices will positively affect the quality of the air element in your home. Hanging wind chimes, mobiles or flags, and decorating with the color yellow are also ways to do this.

Minerals: One of the most soothing ways we can embrace the outdoors is to decorate with minerals - like pink Himalayan salt lamps. These lamps are constructed by placing a light bulb inside a large chunk of pink Himalayan salt. They emit a warming amber glow and create a calming ambience in your home. In addition, some people swear by these lamps to cleanse the air because they are natural ionizers (meaning they alter the electrical charge of the circulating air). Although this has not been scientifically tested, the ambience alone is enough to consider picking up one of these lamps. The pink-amber glow of the lamp mimics the sunset, so dimming the lights at night and recharging in the amber glow can be an impactful way to mitigate all of the artificial blue lights we are bombarded with on a daily basis.

Bamboo: I highly recommend using bamboo textiles in your home when possible. Replacing cotton towels and sheets with this more eco-friendly and less toxic alternative is another way to invite the outdoors into your surroundings. The process of growing and harvesting bamboo is much less invasive than the process used for cotton. Bamboo has always been grown without the use of pesticides and it uses 1/3 of the amount of water. These facts alone make it a smarter investment. Not to mention the fact it is so much softer and stronger than cotton! It is also a self-replenishing resource, and one acre of bamboo yields 10 times more usable textile than one acre of cotton. The top reason I suggest bamboo sheets and towels is because the fabric is hypoallergenic. You will sleep better and wake up more refreshed. You may choose to switch over your towels as well since bamboo is more absorbent that cotton.

3. <u>Use non-toxic cleaning products:</u> Why would we choose to clean our beautiful sanctuary with products that are poisonous? The great part about switching to natural cleaning products is that you might already have many effective cleansing agents. You can make your own using different combinations of apple cider vinegar, essential oils, and baking soda. Tea tree and lavender essential oil can be used for disinfecting; while lemongrass oil can be used in areas like sinks, garbage cans, bathrooms, and garbage disposals. If you don't want to make your own products, try doing a little bit of research on better-for-you brands like Mrs. Meyer's Clean Day or Method.

4. <u>Invest in your comfort:</u> A true sanctuary will be lush and comfortable. Even if your personal style is more streamlined and modern, the furniture you choose should invite comfort. Remember, we want to make your home a place that you look forward to returning to at the end of the day; knowing that comfort awaits is a huge part of this. Invest in pillows, blankets, sofas, and rugs that are snug and cozy. When choosing these items, steer toward natural fabrics such as bamboo.

5. <u>Keep your kitchen stocked with healthy foods and pure water:</u> This is simple, but not always easy. The concept is to make your home a space that fosters growth in all ways, so stocking up on healthy food is an integral part of this. You can make this easier on yourself in a number of different ways. Try pre-cutting and pre-washing your fruits and vegetables, and

keeping them in the front of your refrigerator. Having the menial task of chopping already done makes the desire to eat healthy much greater, and you will meet your health and fitness goals much easier. It has been said many times by many others, but when you keep healthy food at home - you eat healthy food.

The food we chose to consume directly impacts how our bodies perform. We all know we should be eating more fruits, vegetables, plant-based protein, whole grains, and leafy greens; however, few are taking the time to make this a reality. If you want clearer skin and healthier hair - start eating this way. If you want to effortlessly maintain your ideal weight - start eating this way. If you want increased energy, improved physicality, more restful sleep, and more control over your emotions - start eating this way.

Truly, what are you waiting for? When it comes down to it, those of us who want to look and feel our best will take the time to make healthy eating a habit. Make the decision to stop feeding yourself food that does not promote your wellbeing and start investing in yourself.

6. <u>Invest in a home sauna:</u> Bonus sanctuary points for this one. Saunas are an ancient tool used for detoxification. Warming the body via sauna is a tradition rooted in Finnish culture and according to research by the Mayo Clinic - the tradition is rooted in fact. Evidence links sauna usage to several health benefits, including reduction in vascular diseases, neuro-cognitive diseases, and more. Conditions such as arthritis, headache, and the flu can also be managed with the use of a

sauna. Research suggests that the benefits are linked to the effect the sauna has on cardiovascular, circulatory, and immune function. Regular use of a sauna can also soothe tired muscles, relieve mental fatigue, strengthen the immune system, help to maintain healthy skin, relieve allergies and congestion, and assist with kidney function.

I suggest keeping one in the home because you can use it at your leisure, whenever you are able to carve out a little time. Using a sauna activates the body's natural detoxification process - sweating. By taking time daily to sweat, we are allowing our body accelerated detox, thus accelerated tissue repair that ultimately leads to a healthier version of you.

7. <u>Clean up after yourself:</u> Respect yourself enough to set aside time every day to do a quick clean up. Taking 30 minutes to wash and put away dishes, do a batch of laundry, pick up and fold clothing, clean the kitchen and bathroom counters, and more - this will pay dividends as your work adds up and you seem to always be living in a clean space. Plan to do a deeper clean of your home once per week.

♦

PEACE COMES FROM WITHIN. DO NOT SEEK
IT WITHOUT.

-BUDDHA

Chapter Eleven

MEDITATION

At the end of 2018, I spent 30 days in Boca Raton, Florida, studying for my 200hr yoga teacher training certificate. The experience was truly phenomenal, and a milestone in my life that I will never forget. Upon meeting the criteria to graduate from the program, I completed the course with accreditation to teach yoga as well as meditation classes.

An individual meditation practice can and does vary greatly from person to person. In many ways, the term 'mindfulness' has become interchangeable with meditation - meditate while brushing your teeth! While showering! While driving!

While I believe mindfulness is key to living in the present moment and enjoying life, it does not always equal *meditating*.

In the Eight Limbs of Yoga, we learn to steady the mind and come to full concentration on a specific deity, sound, object, phrase (mantra), or movement. This is the 6th limb of yoga, known as *Dharana*. The limbs of yoga are meant to be practiced in succession; each one prepares you for the next. By focusing intently on our breath, gazing into a candle flame or chanting a mantra - *mantra japa* - we can begin to steady the mind and enter a state of pure concentration or Dharana.

For some, a large segment of the 20 minute meditation can be spent in Dharana. One may find at first that only fleeting moments of true meditation or what is known as the 7th limb of yoga - *Dhyana* - may occur. Dhyana is the uninterrupted flow of concentration. In your mind, imagine small drops of smooth oil dripping individually from a glass container. Drop by drop, the oil of concentration flows, until it begins to flow as an even stream. The even and uninterrupted stream is Dhyana.

It is important to remember that every stage of the process is beneficial to our spirituality. We must not try to rush ourselves to the next limb, rather try to acknowledge our progress and live in the present moment.

♦

When practicing meditation, remembering the following habits will enhance your focus:

1. <u>The Place:</u> Maintain a tidy space that will be your meditation room or corner. You will find options below for props you may want to include in this space. In addition, see chapter 10 - *Sacred Space* - for further inspiration for creating a meditation sanctuary.

2. <u>The Time:</u> The most favorable times of day to meditate are dawn and dusk. If you cannot commit to one of these times, commit to a time that does work for you and stay consistent.

3. <u>The Habit:</u> Consistency is key. Try to meditate at the same time every day.

4. <u>The Journal:</u> A meditation journal is an extremely powerful tool. As you grow in your meditation journey you may experience interesting visions, shifts in awareness or perspective, bodily sensations, scents, etc. When we come out of meditation, these experiences are heightened and we think we will remember them. However, the experience quickly fades as we integrate back into the Earthly plane. Use this journal to record the date and anything that happens during your meditation session. Leave nothing out, even if it seems irrelevant, you may look back in a few months to see that it was all part of a specific path.

♦

MEDITATION PROPS

1. <u>Meditation Cushion</u>: The practice of yoga began as a way to cultivate deeper breathing. Thus, if you are not breathing properly - you are not technically practicing yoga (even if you can twist into a pretzel or nail a serious inversion). For this reason, the beginnings of yoga looked like people sitting cross-legged and breathing. Sounds like meditation, right? I recommend a cushion for meditating so that you are able to sit comfortably in Padmasana with an elongated spine. Doing this will greatly enhance your ability to breathe properly.

2. <u>Music and Headphones</u>: Listening to music via headphones is a great way to allow the vibration of sound to guide you deeper into a meditative state. You can find meditation music on YouTube and Spotify for free. I suggest creating a playlist and adding your favorites as you find them.

3. <u>Crystals</u>: We can use crystals to raise our personal vibration and also invite in a certain vibration - such as peace, abundance, strength, love, etc. If you are new to the crystal world, I suggest visiting a metaphysical shop and checking out their crystals. Likely, there will be one that or two catch your attention. You can always ask the shopkeeper for specific crystals if there is a particular vibe you are looking to cultivate. For example, you can choose a rose quartz to cultivate love.

4. <u>Eye Mask</u>: An eye mask is a fantastic aid in reaching a state of concentration. With the eyesight blocked, we are forced to

go within and we cease to be bombarded with external visual stimuli.

5. <u>Oracle Cards</u>: We can use oracle cards to conjure the energy of a specific deity in our mind's eye. Pulling a card before meditation can provide an internal focal point. Pulling a card after meditation may provide insight you can take with you and use throughout the day.

MEDITATION MIST

Supplies

1 amber or blue glass spray bottle
2 ounces witch hazel
1 teaspoon Himalayan pink salt
lavender essential oil
neroli essential oil
rose essential oil
cedar wood essential oil

Method

Step 1: Fill the spray bottle with witch hazel and salt.
Step 2: Add a total of 30 drops essential oil (in whatever combination of oils you prefer).
Step 3: Shake the mixture before each use, and spray your meditation area before each session. **Note:** Use this mist to create a calming effect at any time during the day or night.

♦

TRUE AND EVERLASTING BEAUTY
IS CULTIVATED IN THE MIND.

Chapter Twelve

BEAUTY: A MINDSET

A lthough it is fun to prepare hair treatments and face masques, the essence of beauty is found within. The truth is that everlasting beauty is a mindset. At a certain point in life, I believe, we all must come to the conclusion that beauty really does come from within; it exists within each and every one of us - despite age, physical features, etc. Until we have this awakening, we remain subject to the opinions of others and may 'crowd source' our opinion of our own beauty. We may receive outward praise of our beauty, but still not feel beautiful when we look in the mirror. This goes to show that when it comes to self acceptance, it truly does not matter what other people think. This is why we are meant to be the beholder of our own beauty. It is not wrong to accept yourself. It is not wrong to appreciate your own beauty, in fact, it is essential to do so.

I believe this is especially important for women. We are raised in a society that would like us to believe that our worth is dependent on our physical beauty. The very basis of advertising is built upon the process of companies stripping us of our self worth and then selling it back to us in the form of their products. Completely normal "human body things" like wrinkles, skin texture, etc. have been demonized and we are meant to feel shame about them.

A person who operates from inner beauty is vibrating at a different frequency. We can recognize it when we see it: the eyes are bright, there is a bounce in the step and confidence in the voice. A person who operates from this level has done the inner work; their inner beauty is expanding in every direction.

The transformative processes (Spiritual Alchemy, Eight Limbs of Yoga) that I have discussed in this book both have the end result of realizing we are one with the Divine. How can we do that when we choose to ignore our own beauty? Or doubt the existence of it altogether?

The same Divine energy that created the natural beauty of the beaches, mountains, flowers, sunrises and sunsets of our world - created you. To admit to your own beauty is to bow to your creator. Honoring yourself with wonderful healthy food and physical exercise is to bow to your creator. Working through problematic mindsets in order to fully realize your own beauty is to bow to your creator. Honoring your own unique talents and living up to your potential is to bow to your creator.

We are beautiful when we hug a friend, when we cook a delicious meal for our family, and when we cuddle our pets. We are beautiful when we take a chance on chasing a dream and when we work toward our goals. We are beautiful in candlelight across from someone we love and we are beautiful walking barefoot in a park. We are beautiful when we smile at a stranger instead of staring at our phone. We are beautiful when we are 25 years old and we are beautiful at 100.

I would like to point out that we take excellent care of the things we love. We take such tender care of the people and things in our life that are precious to us. The good news is, you do not have to wait until you love yourself to take care of yourself. In fact, if you do not see your own beauty, taking better care of yourself is the perfect way to begin. If you do not yet love yourself, the only way to get there is to start taking care of your mind, body, and spirt.

That is what this book is, a guide for you to learn how to take care of someone you love: Yourself.

◆

<u>NOTES</u>

<u>NOTES</u>

NOTES

BIBLIOGRAPHY

Literary Works

1. Zen Den Yoga School. 2013. *Yoga Teacher Training Manual.* Boca Raton, Florida.

2. Hill, Dennis. 2008. *Yoga Sutras: The Means to Liberation.* Bloomington, Indiana: Trafford Publication.

3. Gunther, Helena. 2006. *Apple Cider Vinegar: History and Folklore - Composition - Medical Research - Medicinal, Cosmetic, and Household Uses - Commercial and Home Production.* Lincoln, Nebraska: iUniverse.

4. Frazier, Karen. 2015. *Crystals for Healing: The Complete Reference Guide.* Berkeley, California: Althea Press.

5. Warwick, Tarl. 2016. *The Greater Key of Solomon: The Grimoire of Solomon.* Columbia, South Carolina.

Digital Resources & Medical Journals

1. Banyan Botanicals. **"The Four Varieties of Agni."** Last modified 2019. <https://www.banyanbotanicals.com/info/ayurvedic-living/living-ayurveda/health-guides/understanding-agni/the-four-varieties-of-agni/>

2. Rishikul Yogahala. **"Top 10 Excellent Benefits of Sun Salutations."** Last modified January 27, 2018. <https://www.rishikulyogshala.org/top-10-excellent-benefits-of-sun-salutations>

3. Medical News Today. **"How to Use Rosemary Oil for Hair Growth."** Last modified September 17, 2017. <https://www.medicalnewstoday.com/articles/319444.php>

4. Aztec Secret Indian Healing Clay. **"History of Healing Clay."** Last modified 2019. <https://aztec-secret.com/history>

5. Paula's Choice Skincare. **"Alpha Hydroxy Acids (AHAs) for Skin: What They Are, How They Work."** No date of modification or publication. <https://www.paulaschoice.com/expert-advice/skincare-advice/anti-aging-wrinkles/alpha-hydroxy-acids-skin-what-they-are-how-they-work.html>

6. PubMed US National Library of Medicine/National Institutes of Health. **"Polyphenols: Food Sources and Bioavailability."** Last modified May 2004. <https://www.ncbi.nlm.nih.gov/pubmed/15113710>

7. PubMed US National Library of Medicine/National Institutes of Health. **"Hydroxycinnamic Acid Antioxidants: An Electrochemical Overview."** Last modified July 2013. <https://www.ncbi.nlm.nih.gov/pubmed/23956973>

8. Gale Encyclopedia of Alternative Medicine. **"Castor Oil."** Last modified July 9, 2019. <https://www.encyclopedia.com/science-and-technology/chemistry/organic-chemistry/castor-oil>

9. PubMed US National Library of Medicine/National Institutes of Health. **"Rosemary Oil vs. Minoxidil 2% For the Treatment of Androgenetic Alopecia: A Randomized Comparative Trial."** Last modified February 2015. <https://www.ncbi.nlm.nih.gov/pubmed/25842469>

10. PubMed US National Library of Medicine/National Institutes of Health Bookshelf. Benzie IFF, Wachtel-Galor S, editors. 2011. *Herbal Medicine: Biomolecular and Clinical Aspects. 2nd Edition.* Boca Raton, Florida: CRC Press/Taylor & Francis <https://www.ncbi.nlm.nih.gov/books/NBK92765/>

11. Research Gate. **"Medical and Cosmetological Importance of Aloe Vera."** Last modified January 2009. <https://www.researchgate.net/publication/233818204_Medicinal_and_cosmetological_importance_of_Aloe_vera>

12. PubMed US National Library of Medicine/National Institutes of Health. **"Comparative Evaluation of Antiplaque Efficacy of Coconut Oil Pulling and a Placebo, Among Dental College Students: A Randomized Controlled Trial."** Last modified September 11, 2017. <https://www.ncbi.nlm.nih.gov/pubmed/29207824>

13. PubMed US National Library of Medicine/National Institutes of Health. **"Antimicrobial Property of Lauric Acid Against Propionibacterium Acnes: Its Therapeutic Potential for Inflammatory Acne Vulgaris."** Last modified April 23, 2009. <https://www.ncbi.nlm.nih.gov/pubmed/19387482>

14. PubMed US National Library of Medicine/National Institutes of Health. **"Comparative Evaluation of 0.1% Turmeric Mouthwash with 0.2% Chlorhexidine Gluconate in Prevention of Plaque and Gingivitis: A Clinical and Microbiological Study."** Last modified September 2012. <https://www.ncbi.nlm.nih.gov/pmc/articles/PMC3498709/>

15. PubMed US National Library of Medicine/National Institutes of Health. **"Magnesium in Prevention and Therapy."** Last modified September 2015. <https://www.ncbi.nlm.nih.gov/pubmed/26404370>

16. PubMed US National Library of Medicine/National Institutes of Health. **"Magnesium in Depression."** Last modified 2013. <https://www.ncbi.nlm.nih.gov/pubmed/23950577>

17. PubMed US National Library of Medicine/National Institutes of Health. **"Pharmacological Effects of *Rosa Damascena*."** Last modified August 2011. <https://www.ncbi.nlm.nih.gov/pmc/articles/PMC3586833/>

18. Anzac Day Commemoration Committee. **"Rosemary is for Remembrance."** No date of modification or publication. <https://anzacday.org.au/rosemary-is-for-remembrance>

19. Esoteric Oils. **"Rosemary Essential Oil Information."** Last modified July 4, 2019. <https://essentialoils.co.za/essential-oils/rosemary.htm>

20. Psychology Today. **"Benefits of the Indoor Plant."** Last modified February 16, 2018. <https://www.psychologytoday.com/us/blog/people-places-and-things/201802/benefits-the-indoor-plant>

21. Mayo Clinic Proceedings. **"Cardiovascular and Other Health Benefits of Sauna Bathing: A Review of the Evidence."** Last modified August 2018. <https://www.mayoclinicproceedings.org/article/S0025-6196(18)30275-1/fulltext>

22. US National Library of Medicine/Genetics Home Reference. **"Androgenetic Alopecia."** Last modified August 2015. <https://ghr.nlm.nih.gov/condition/androgenetic-alopecia>

23. PubMed US National Library of Medicine/National Institutes of Health. **"Suboptimal Magnesium Status in the United States: Are the Health Consequences Underestimated?"** Last modified March 2012. <https://www.ncbi.nlm.nih.gov/pubmed/22364157>

FURTHER READING RECOMMENDATIONS

If you enjoyed the topics in this book, you may enjoy the following books as well.

The Alchemist by Paulo Coehlo

The Celestine Prophecy by James Redfield

Moon Juice Cook Book by Amanda Chantal Bacon

Tuning the Human Biofield by Eileen Day McKusick

The Power of Now by Eckhart Tolle

The Hidden Messages in Water by Masaru Emoto

The Greater Key of Solomon edited by Tarl Warwick

Yoga Sutras translation and commentary by Dennis Hill

Eat Pretty Everyday by Jolene Hart

The Magician's Companion by Bill Whitcomb

The Golden Secrets to Optimal Health by Jesse Golden

Egyptian Yoga by Muata Ashby

The Paris Bath & Beauty Book by Chrissy Callahan

ACKNOWLEDGMENTS

My husband, Ross, thank you for being the greatest partner in life that I could ask for. I feel fortunate beyond measure to grow and learn together, as we transform into our best versions. Thank you for believing in me every single day and I will never take our open communication or your sunny perspective for granted. I love you.

Ashley, for showing me a world where Ancient Egyptian queens are still relevant and raw vegan food is the most delicious.

Callie, for being the kind of friend that every person should be lucky enough to have.

Marcus and Chaffin, for existing with me in this life, past lives, and future ones.

ABOUT THE AUTHOR

Valerie Cody is a certified and registered yoga teacher who specializes in the Sivananda-Hatha tradition as well as Ashtanga inspired vinyasa. She earned her B.A. in Communications with an emphasis on journalism and public relations from Waldorf College in 2011. In 2016, she earned her certification in Plant-Based Nutrition from eCornell. In December 2018, she completed her yoga teacher training at Zen Den Yoga School in Boca Raton, Florida, after which she become qualified to teach yoga and meditation techniques.

She lives in North Carolina with her husband, Ross; her dachshund, Sundae; and her black cat, Bellatrix.

◆

Made in the USA
Columbia, SC
07 August 2019